Good Morning, Words!

HarperCollinsPublishers

Part of this dictionary is also published under the title *My Pictionary.*

D'Nealian is the registered trademark of Donald Neal Thurber.

First HarperCollins edition published 1991

Illustration and photograph credits appear on page 143.

Library of Congress Cataloging-in-Publication Data

Good morning, words!
p. cm.
Reprint. Originally published: Glenview, Ill. : Scott Foresman, 1990.
Summary: Illustrates words in such categories as people, places, things, animals, and opposites.
ISBN 0-06-275000-3
1. Vocabulary—Juvenile literature. [1. Vocabulary.]
PE1449.G575 1991
428.1—dc20
90-42739

91 92 93 94 95 RRW 10 9 8 7 6 5 4 3 2 1

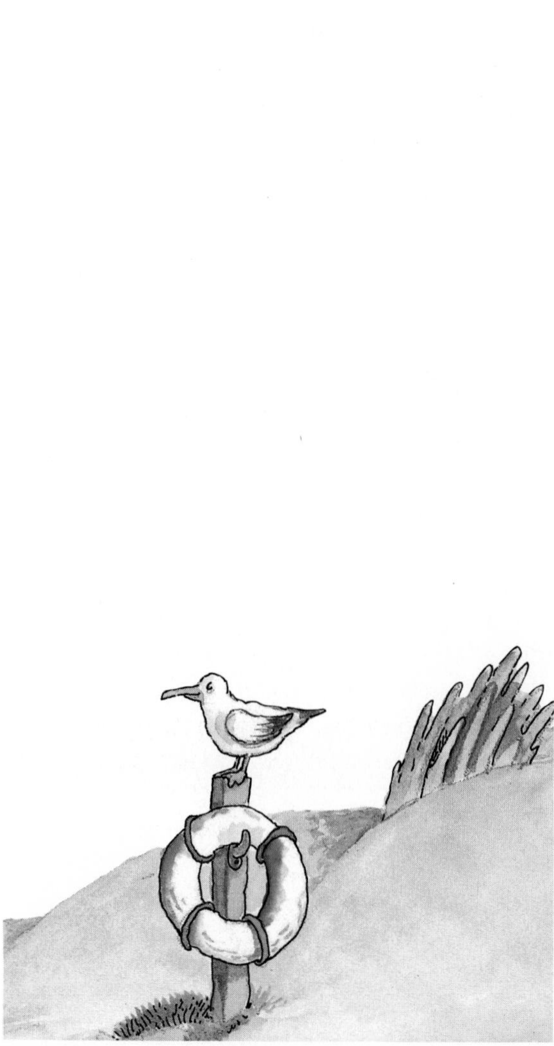

Introduction: For the Parent

Good Morning, Words! is a picture wordbook for children who are just learning to read and write. It is a colorful, fun-filled way to take the first rewarding steps into reading and writing.

The words in *Good Morning, Words!* are arranged in categories familiar to children. All too often our language is unfamiliar to children and even bewildering. Many words, such as *eight* and *ate,* are pronounced alike but are spelled differently. Other words do not sound anything like the way they are spelled. In fact, our alphabet has twenty-six letters to represent more than forty sounds. So it is easy to see why young children have trouble in deciding what letter a word begins with and why they often struggle in finding a word in a long alphabetical list.

The categories in this book group words according to their meaning and function. The words grouped under **People, Animals, Places,** and **Things** are nouns; those under **What We Do** are verbs; and those grouped as **Opposites** and **Helping Words** are adjectives and prepositions. To find a word, a child need only ask, "What kind of word is it?" Then he or she can find the word, along with others like it, under the proper heading. Each category is also color-coded and has a distinct visual style for easy reference.

Every word in *Good Morning, Words!* has a picture carefully selected to represent that word. Some pictures even have labels printed in smaller type to identify additional aspects of the picture, such as *feather* and *wing* for **eagle.**

The 850 entries in *Good Morning, Words!* were chosen from a list made up of words, images, and concepts that children will encounter in kindergarten. Current trade books (fiction and nonfiction) and other kindergarten materials (texts on reading, language arts, handwriting, science, health, mathematics, and social studies) were examined in detail to make up the word list. In addition to these words children encounter at school are the names of things commonly found in their homes and neighborhoods.

Published by Scott, Foresman and Company, a leader for more than fifty years in producing quality children's dictionaries, *Good Morning, Words!* was prepared by an experienced team of editors, designers, and illustrators. A panel of primary teachers also served as project advisors throughout the development of this book.

Research has shown that children who do well in school are those who are given a head start in reading at home. Looking through books and oral reading are important steps in creating a head start for a child. You can help simply by taking time to read to your child—pointing out words and pictures and talking about what you read.

For hints on reading *Good Morning, Words!* with your child, please turn to the inside back cover. We hope you and your child spend many happy hours reading this book.

Contents

Contents

Letters of the Alphabet

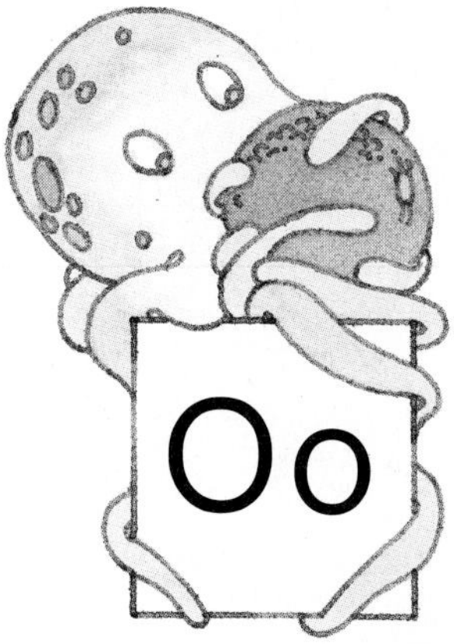

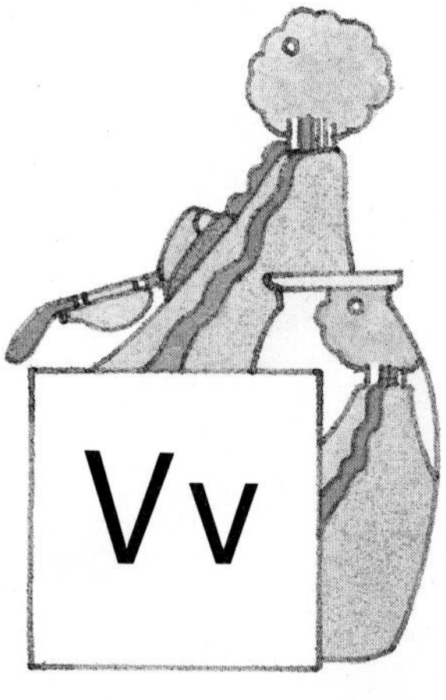

Letters of the Alphabet

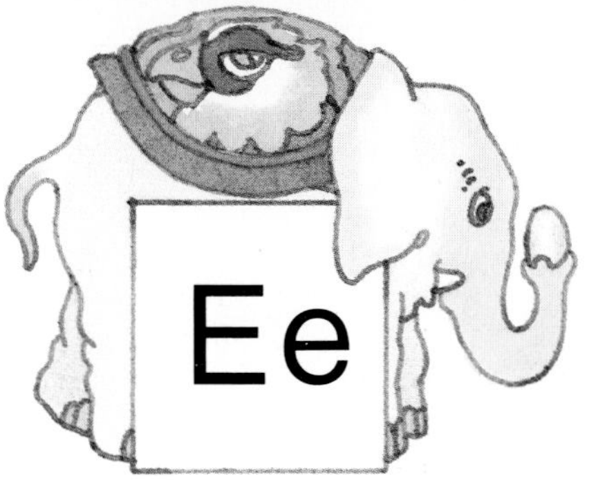

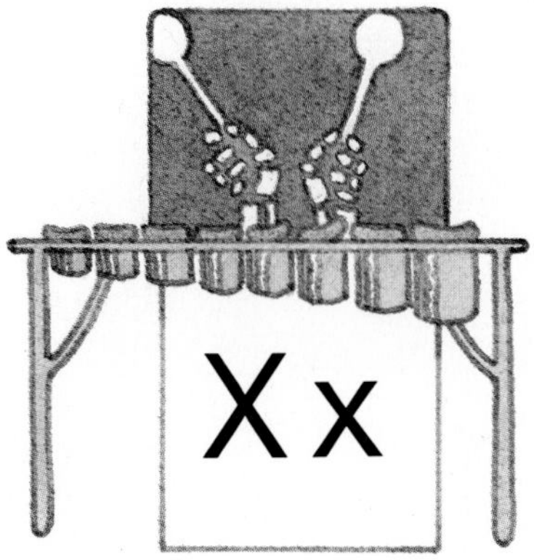

People

adults

grown-ups

child

children

woman

women

People

friends

man

men

baby

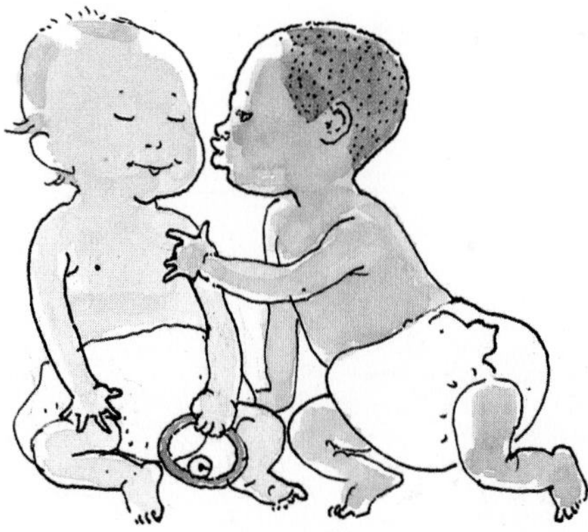

babies

twins

People: Family

grandmother
mother
mom
mama
son
boy
grandfather

People: The Work People Do / Jobs

clown

policewoman

police officers

policeman

salesperson

teacher

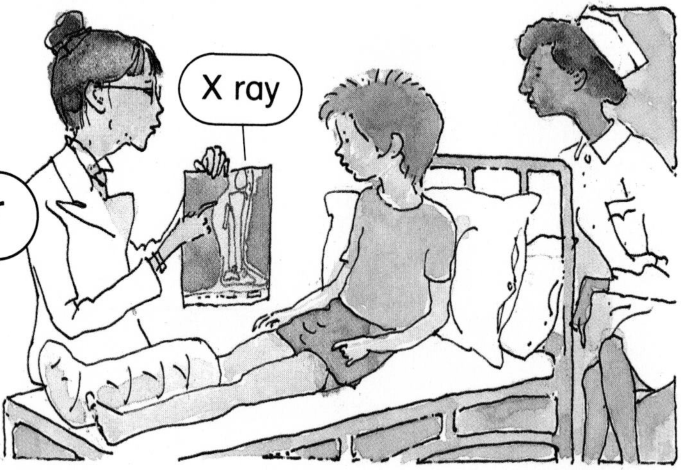

doctor

nurse

astronaut
judge
lawyer
cowboy
baker

People: The Work People Do / Jobs

painter

plumber

electrician

photographer

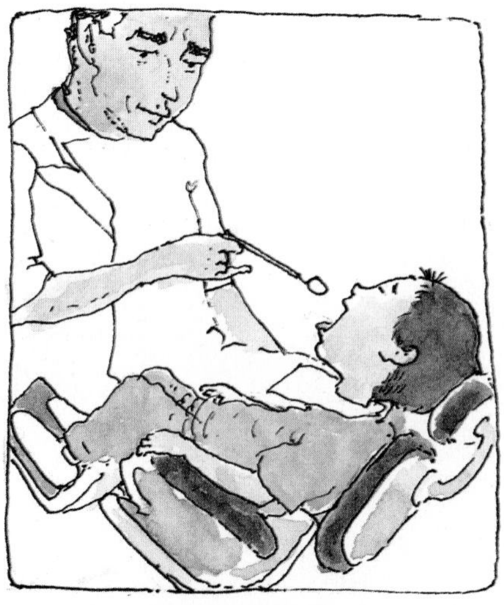

dentist

librarian

People: The Work People Do / Jobs

firefighter

mail carrier

soldier

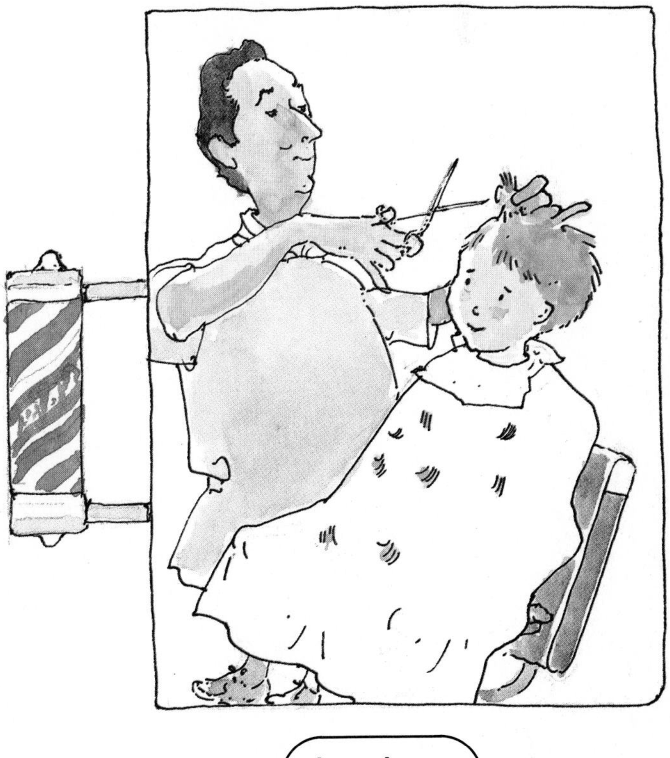

barber

People: The Work People Do / Jobs

farmer
artist
factory worker

People: The Parts of the Body

hair
finger
ear
eye
nose
lip
teeth
chin
neck
chest

Animals: Pets

dog

puppy

puppies

parakeet

parrot

goldfish

guinea pig

bunny

kitten

hamster

gerbil

lamb sheep

sheep

chickens

turkey

hen

chick

rooster

cow
calf

pig
hog

horse
pony
colt

donkey

goat

groundhog

raccoon

wolf

beaver

skunk

coyote

chipmunk

squirrel

fox

foxes

Animals: Wild Animals

porcupine

mouse

mice

deer

deer

possum

opossum

bat

polar bear

panda

bear

rat

kangaroo

turtle

snake

alligator

lizard

iguana

spider

fish

lobster

frog

toad

seal

octopus

walrus

whale

dolphin

chimpanzee

ape

gorilla

ape

monkey

monkeys

lion

tiger

leopard

yak

camel

giraffe

zebra

elephant

rhinoceros

hippopotamus

Animals: Birds

goose

geese

ostrich

crow

blue jay

Animals: Birds

eagle

owl

robin

hummingbird

cardinal

duck

Animals: Insects / Bugs

ant

butterfly

caterpillar

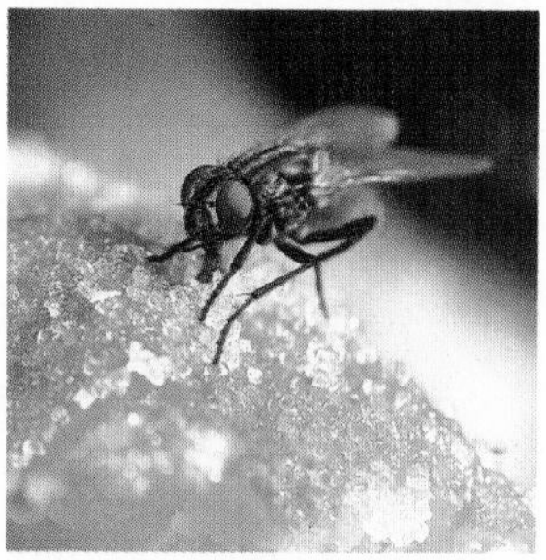

fly

beetle

bee

stegosaurus

iguanodon

ankylosaurus

ornitholestes

tyrannosaurus

triceratops

apatosaurus

brachiosaurus

Storybook Characters

Storybook Characters

Places: Home

attic
bathroom
bedroom
kitchen
dining room
house
basement

garden
roof
doghouse
fence
gate
living room
mailbox
yard
sidewalk

Places: The City

hospital
park
LIONS
zoo

Places: The City

Places: The City

farm
barn
silo
pigpen

field
tractor
hay
meadow

Places: The Country

country
continent
world
earth

Things: Food

fruit

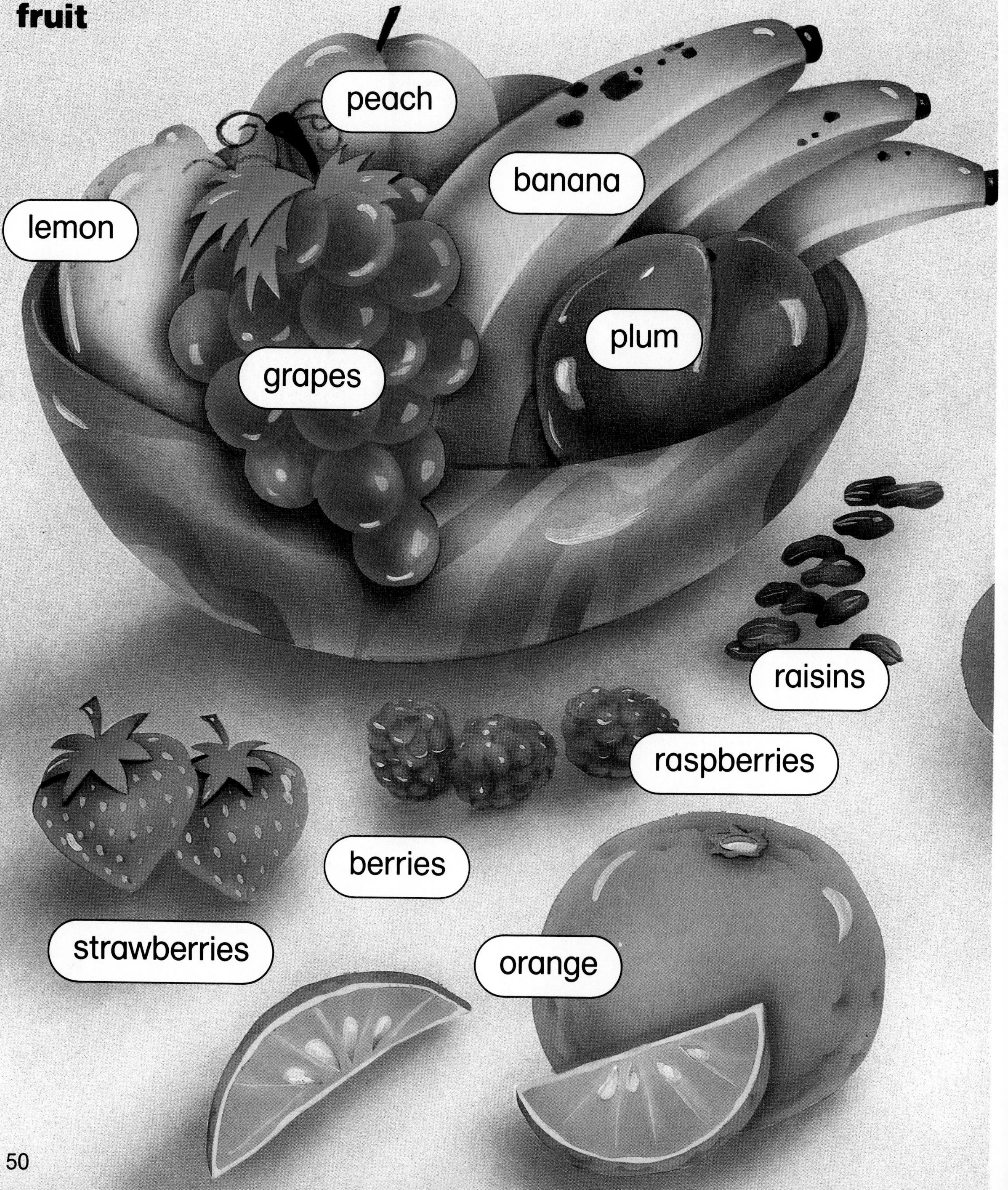

cherries
pear
apple
watermelon
tomatoes
tomato

vegetables

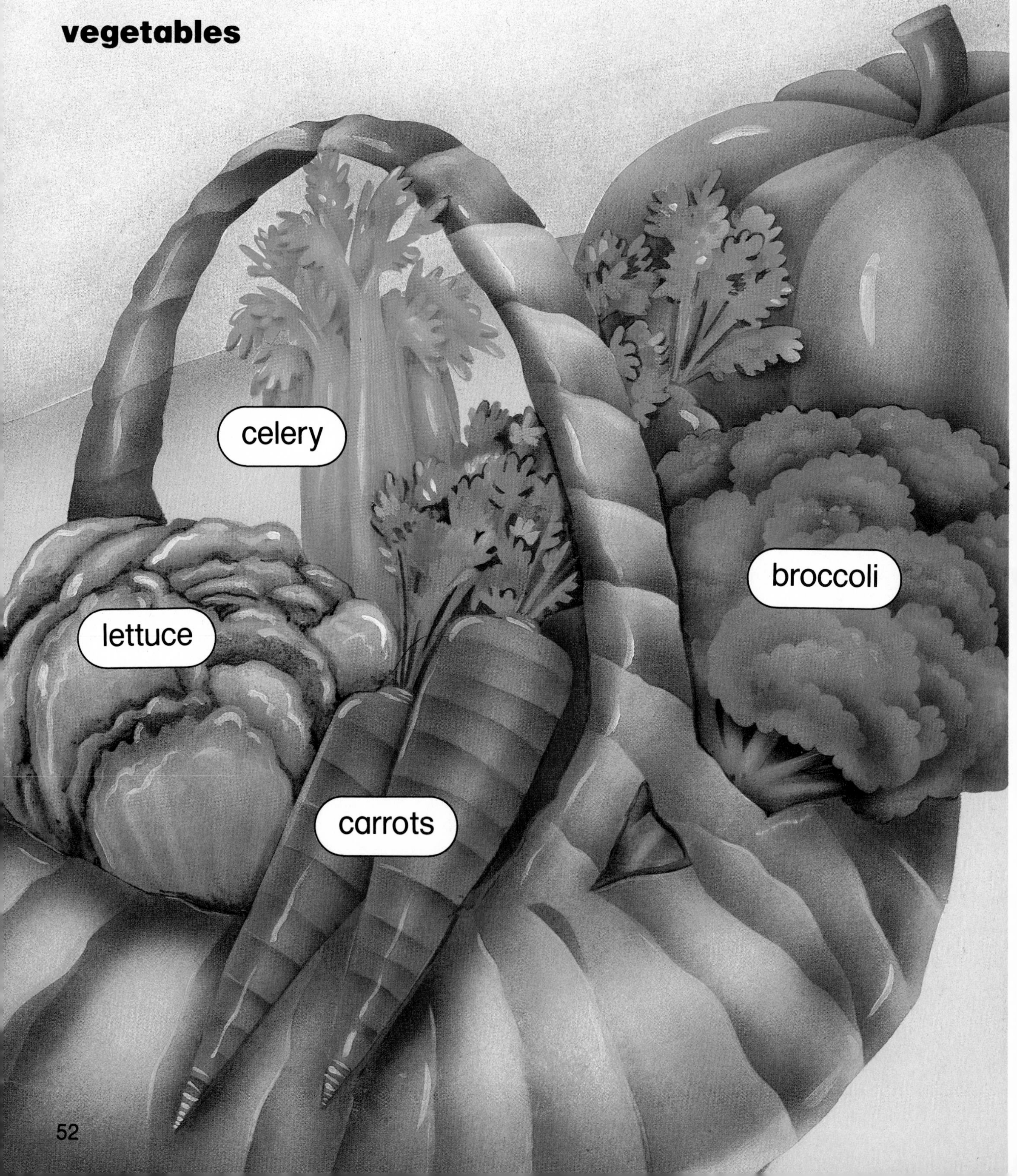

potato
pumpkin
potatoes
corn
beets
beans
peas

Things: Food

peanut butter
sandwich
cheese
meat
candy
pie

Things: Food

honey
bread
cereal
pancakes
butter

Things: Food

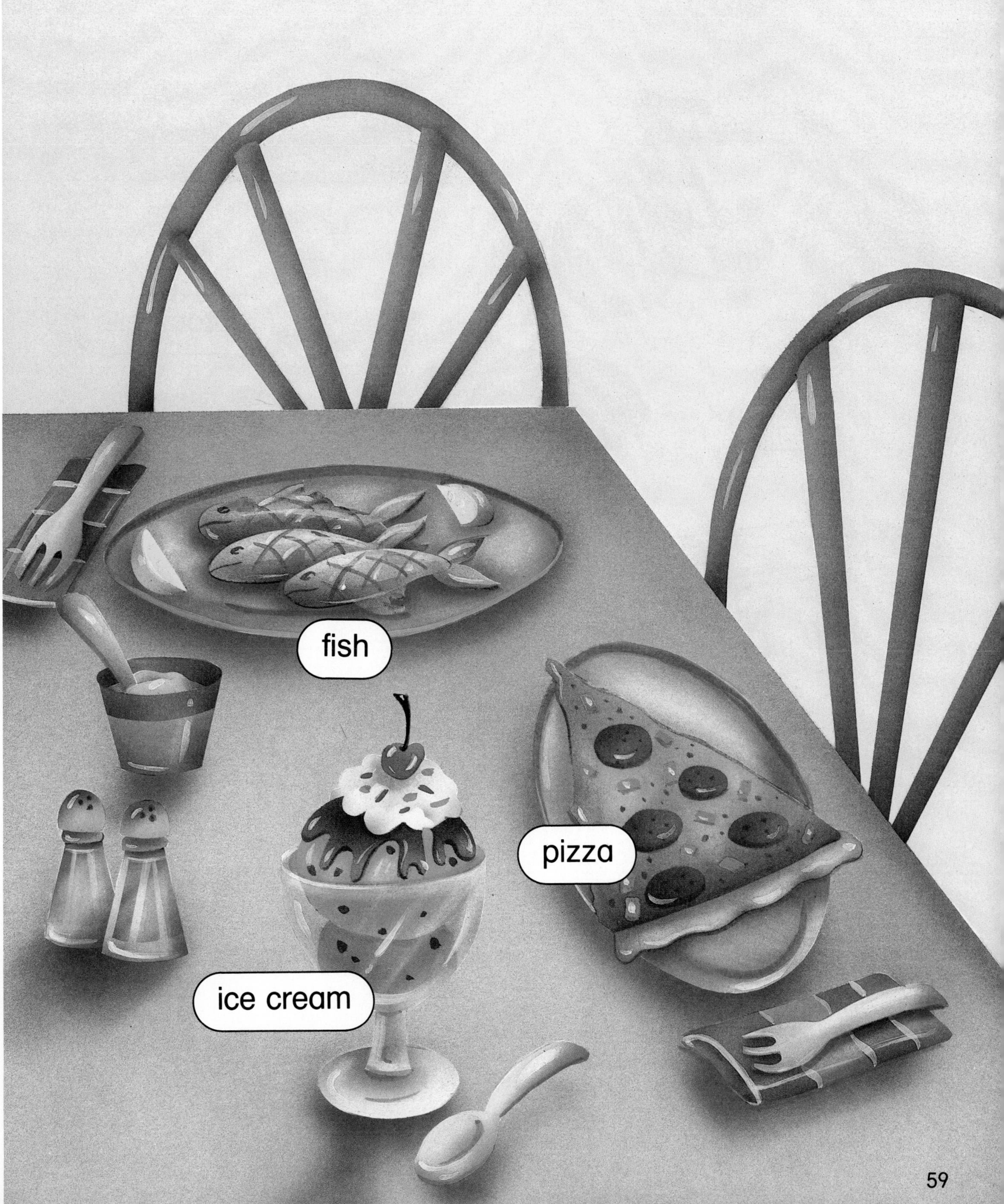
fish
pizza
ice cream

Things: Things We Ride In

Things: Things We Ride In

Things: Things We Ride In

ship

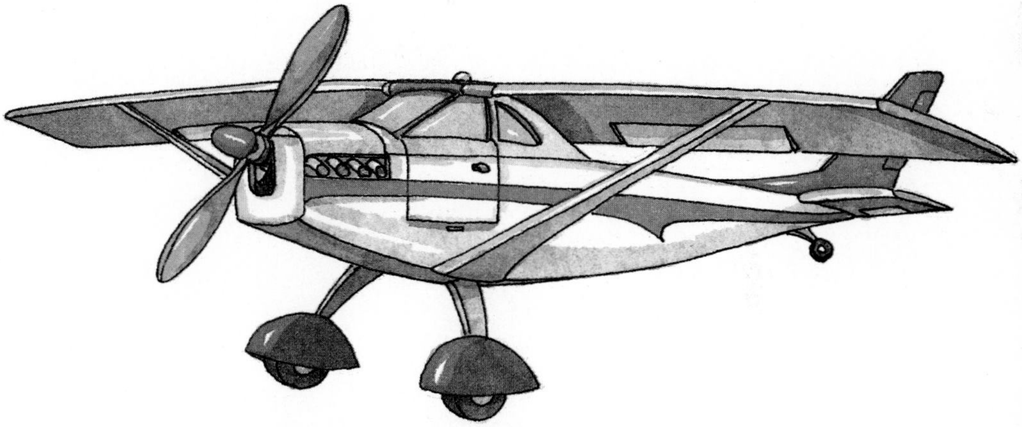
airplane
plane

fire engine
fire truck
FD

Things: Things Around the House

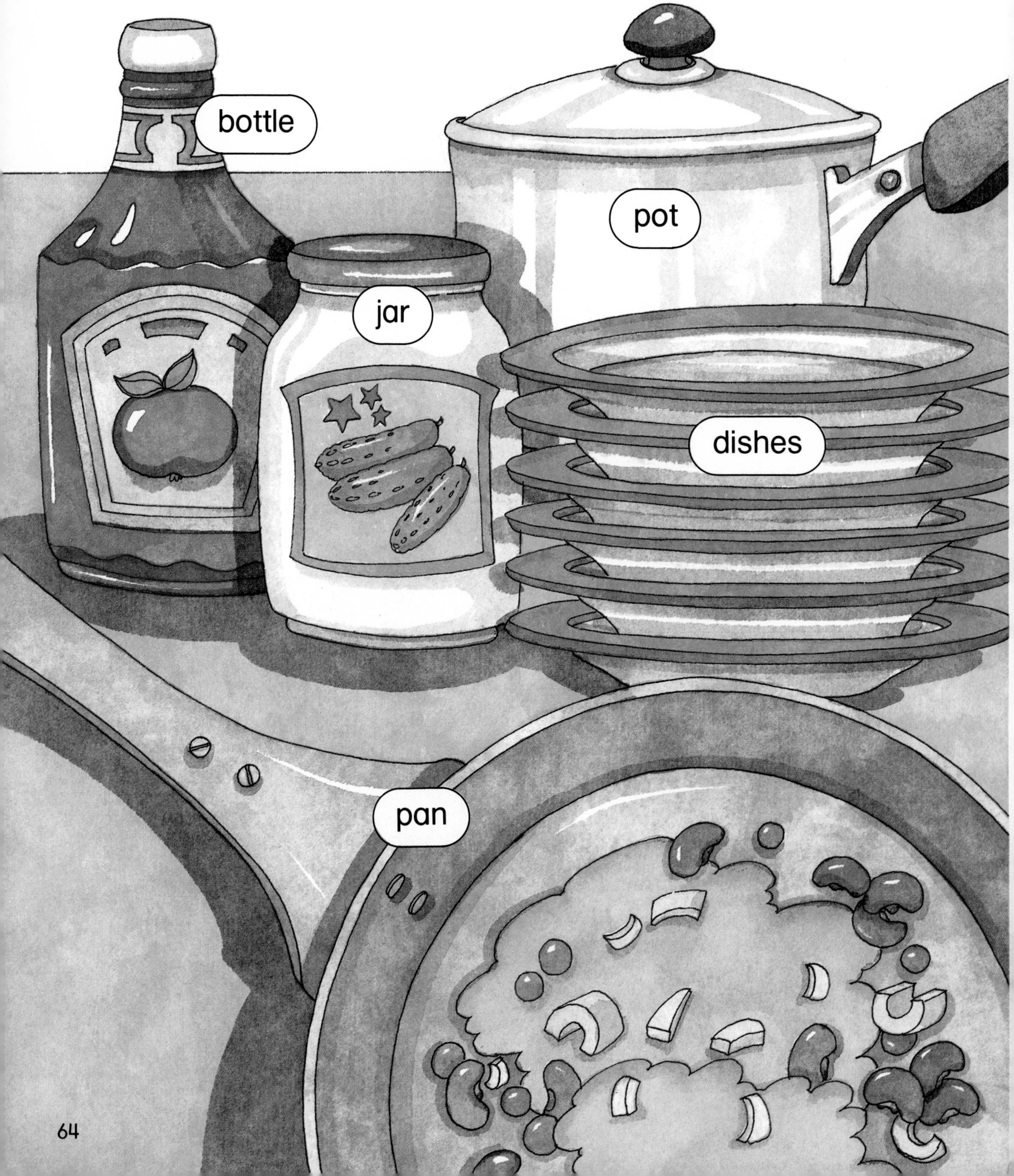

bowl
glass
cup
napkin
plate
fork
knife
spoon

Things: Things Around the House

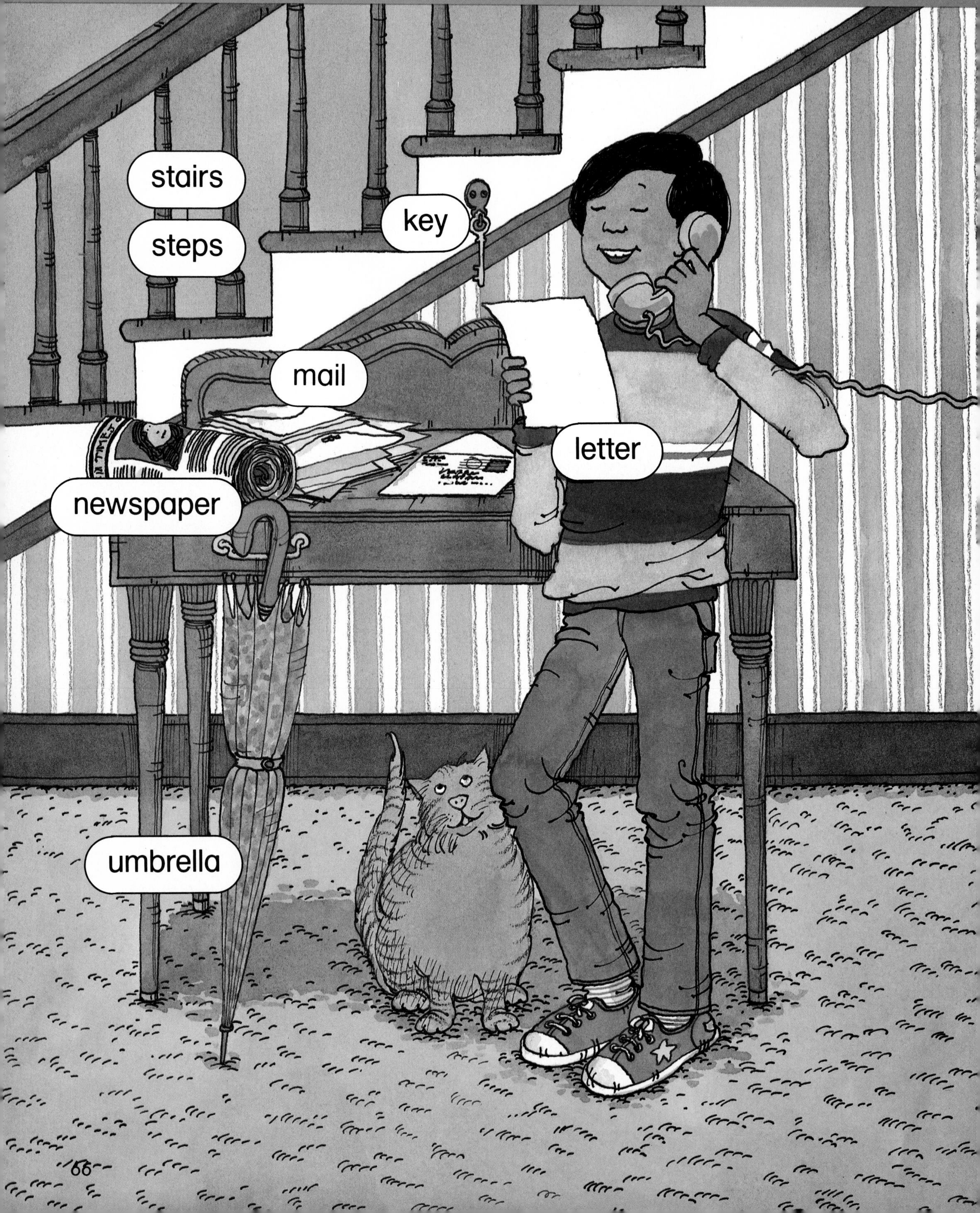

picture
lamp
telephone
phone
computer
chair
desk

Things: Things Around the House

groceries
refrigerator
table
DUFFY
bag
box

Things: Things Around the House

curtains
window
crib
straight pin
yarn
safety pin

Things: Things Around the House

saw
rake
nail
washing machine
washer
dryer

Things: Classroom Things

chalkboard
AaBbCcDdEe
Susan
name
flag
easel
chalk
RED
BLUE
GREEN
paint

Things: Clothes / Clothing

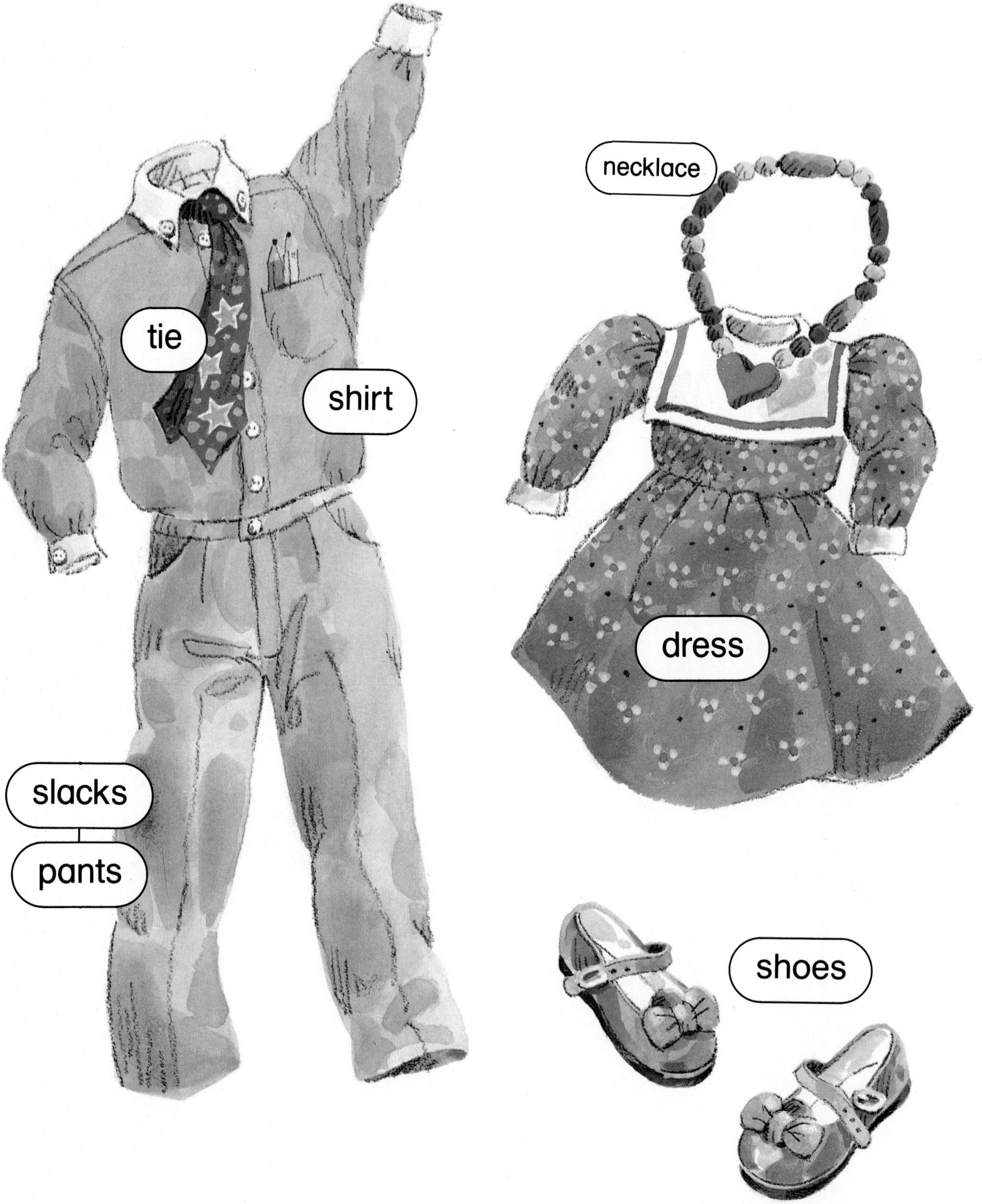

vest
sweater
button
pocket
skirt
jeans

gloves
cap
mittens
coat
zipper
jacket
scarf

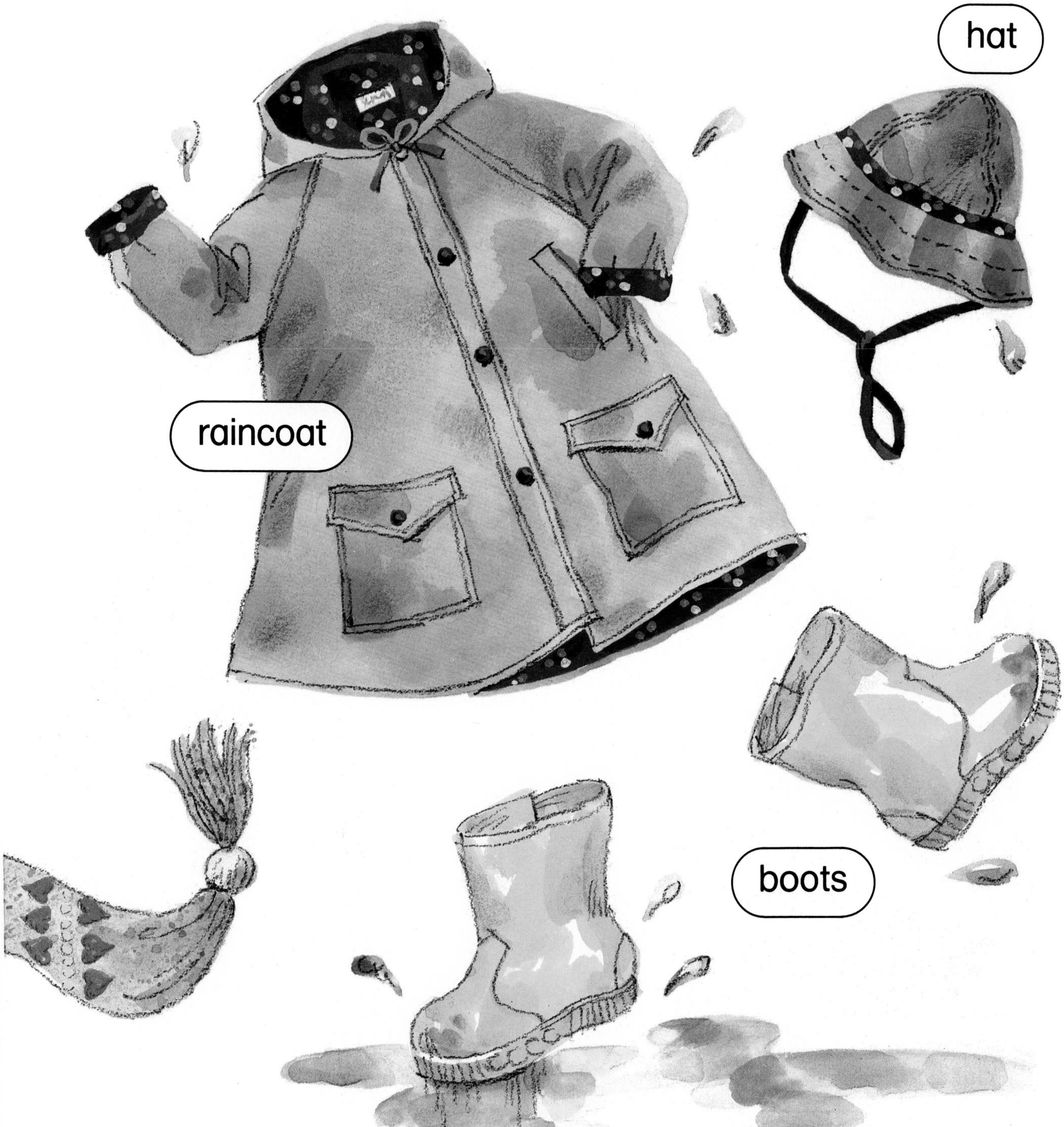
hat
raincoat
boots

Things: Clothes / Clothing

watch

pajamas

ring

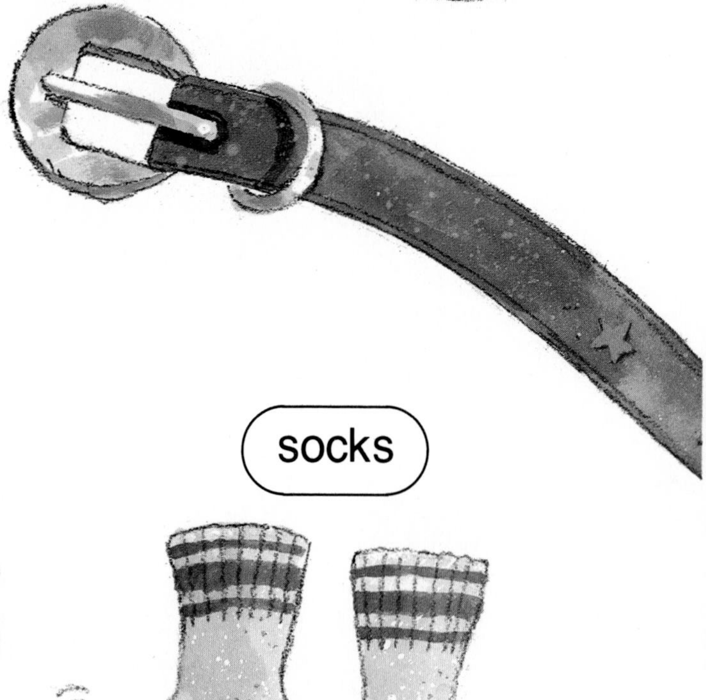

socks

bathing suit

T-shirt

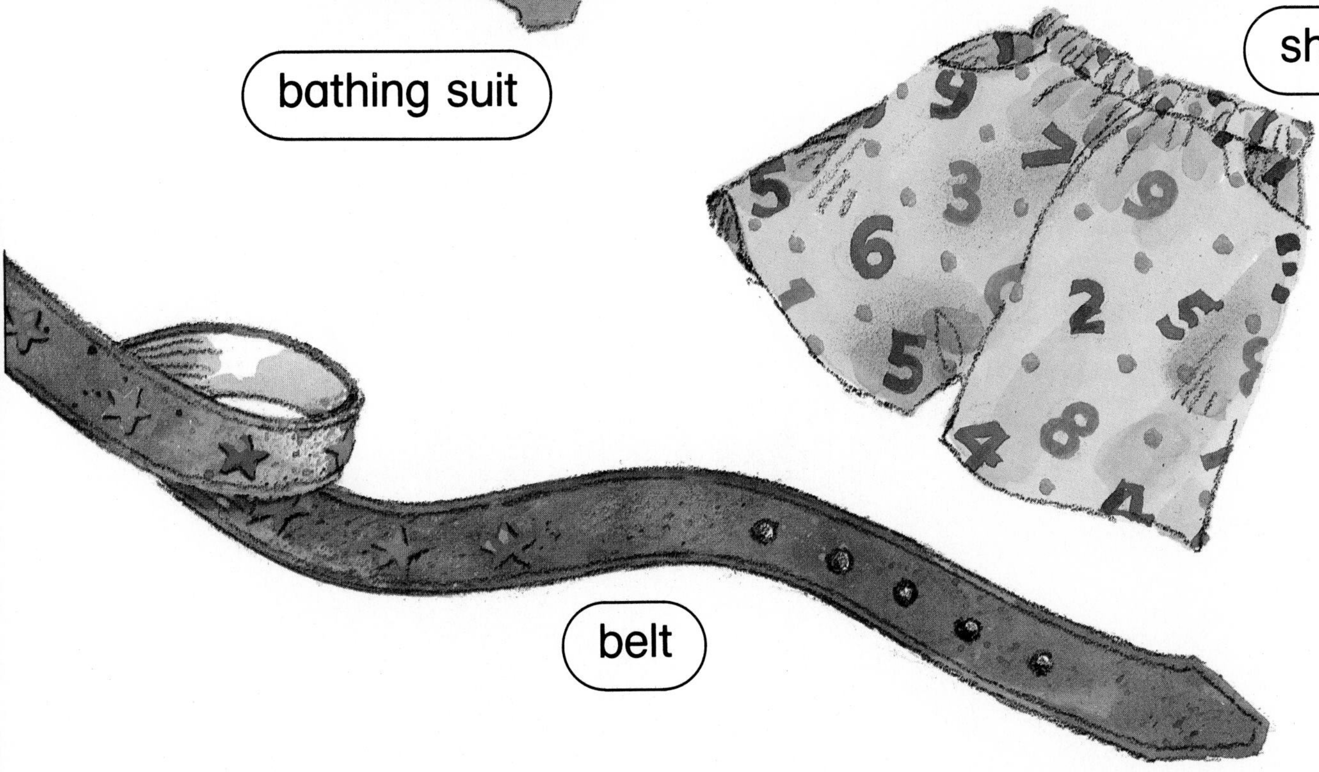

shorts

belt

wind
land
grass
fire
stick

rainbow
volcano
island
water
ocean
sea
seeds
beach
shell
eggshell
turtle's shell
nutshell
seashell

Things: Things in Nature

lightning
river
stream
plant
stem
vine
mushroom
root
pond

desert

cloud
sky
rock
stone
shadow

Things: Things in Nature

moon
stars
lake

toys

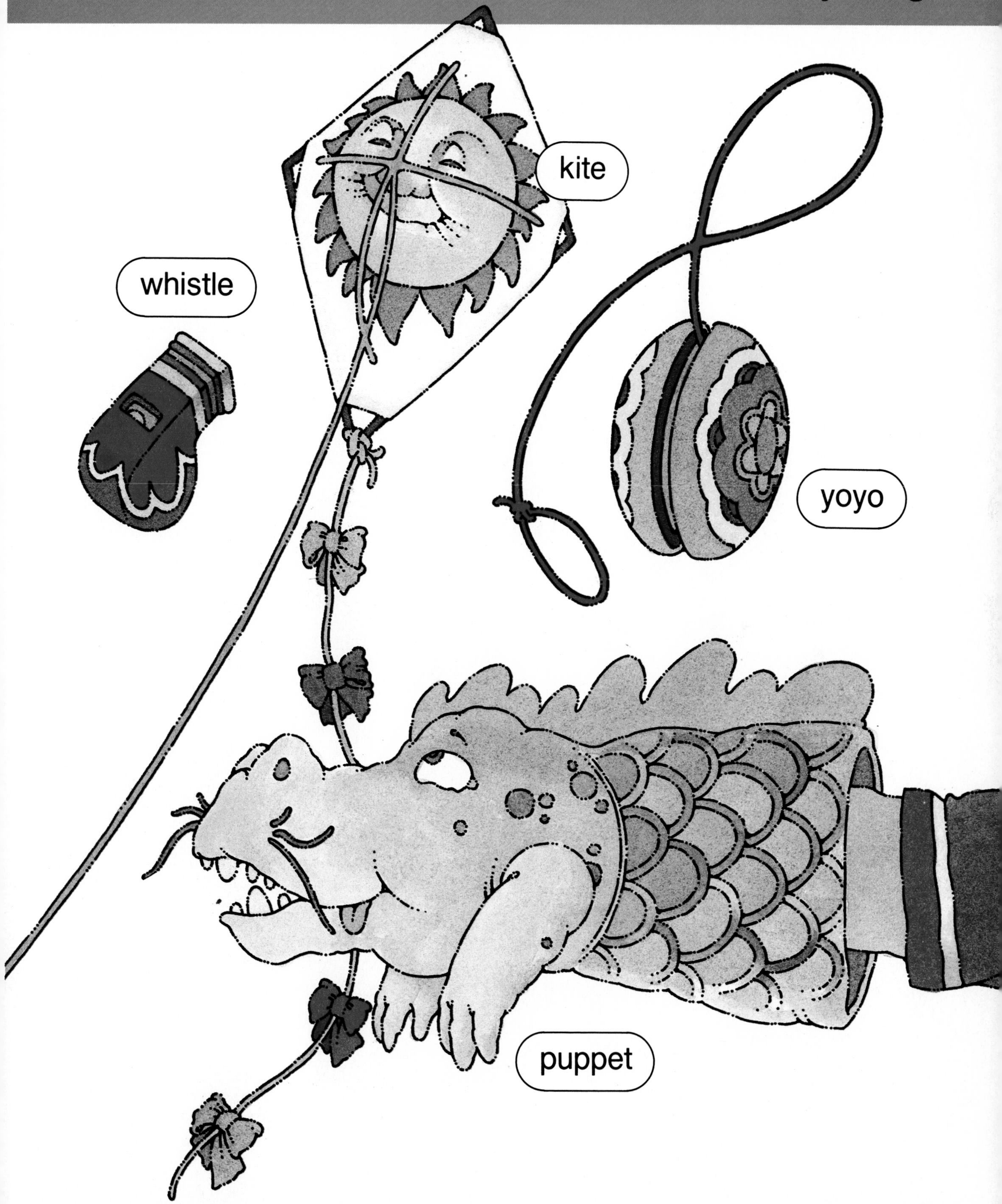
kite
whistle
yoyo
puppet

Things: Playthings

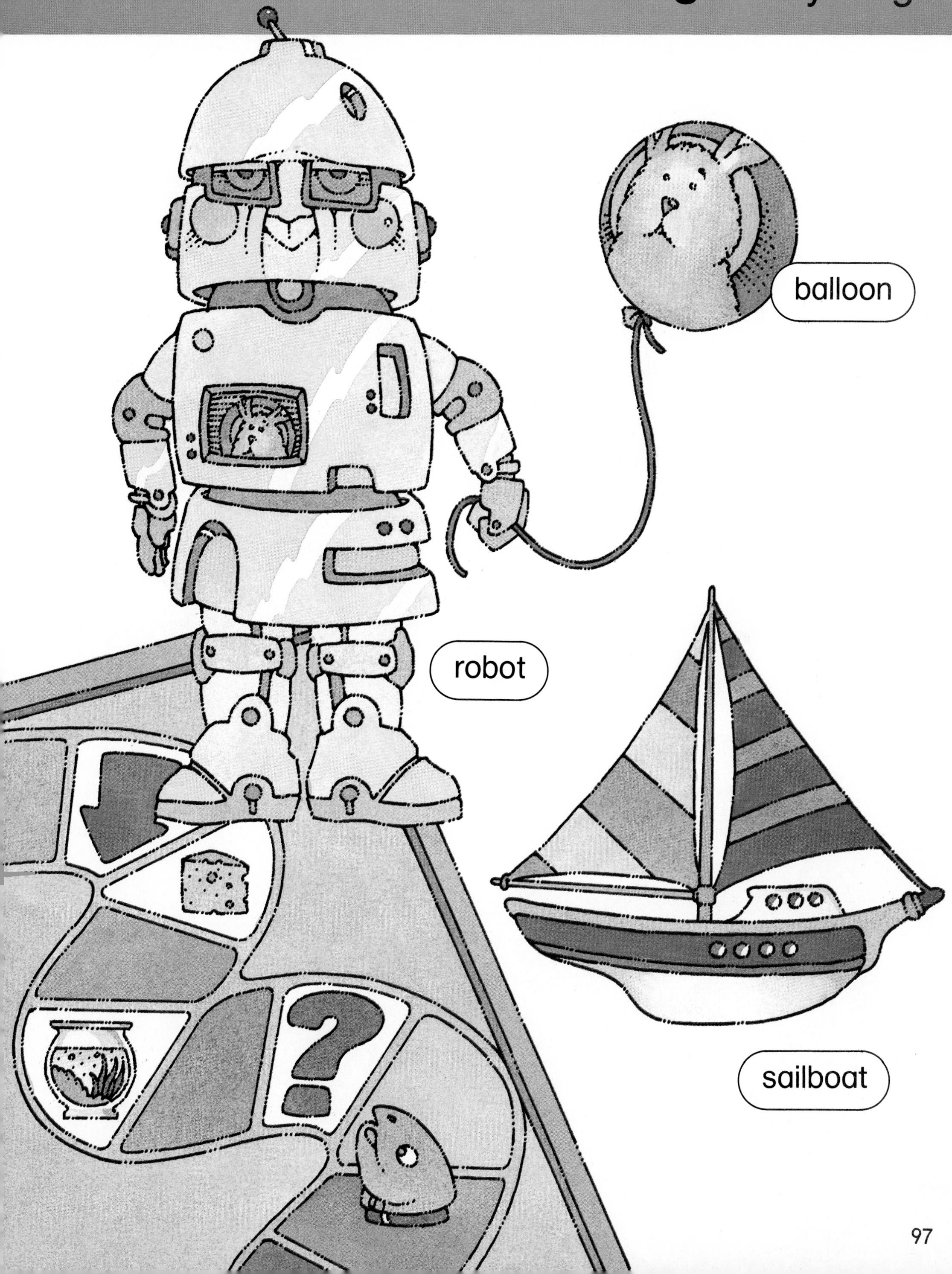
balloon
robot
sailboat

swings
slide
seesaw
sandbox
dump truck

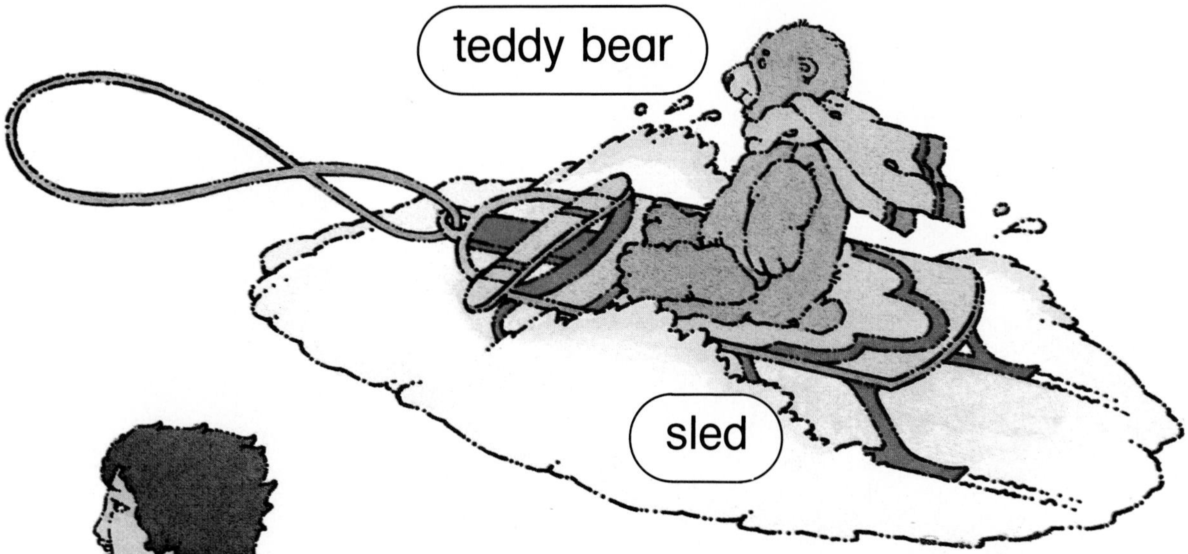
teddy bear
sled

skates
roller skates

ice skates

tricycle

guitar
bells
drum
violin

horn
xylophone
piano

Things: Sports

picnic

birthday
party
present

parade

play

circus

What We Do

What We Do

What We Do

What We Do

What We Do

What We Do

TWO GUYS AND ONE TRUCK - MOVERS --
moving van
move
saw
hammer
paint

What We Do

What We Do

What We Do

What We Do

What We Do

What We Do

What We Do

draw
cut
fold
color
watch
sit
trace
paste

Opposites

in front of
in back of
ahead
behind
GAS
to
from

Opposites

light — dark

day — night

alike — different

same

old — new

big — little

large — tiny

small

Opposites

Opposites

Opposites

Opposites

up
down
fast
slow
hard
soft

Helping Words

top
at
middle
bottom
into
in

Colors

blue
red
brown
gray
white
pink
yellow
black
green
orange
purple

Shapes

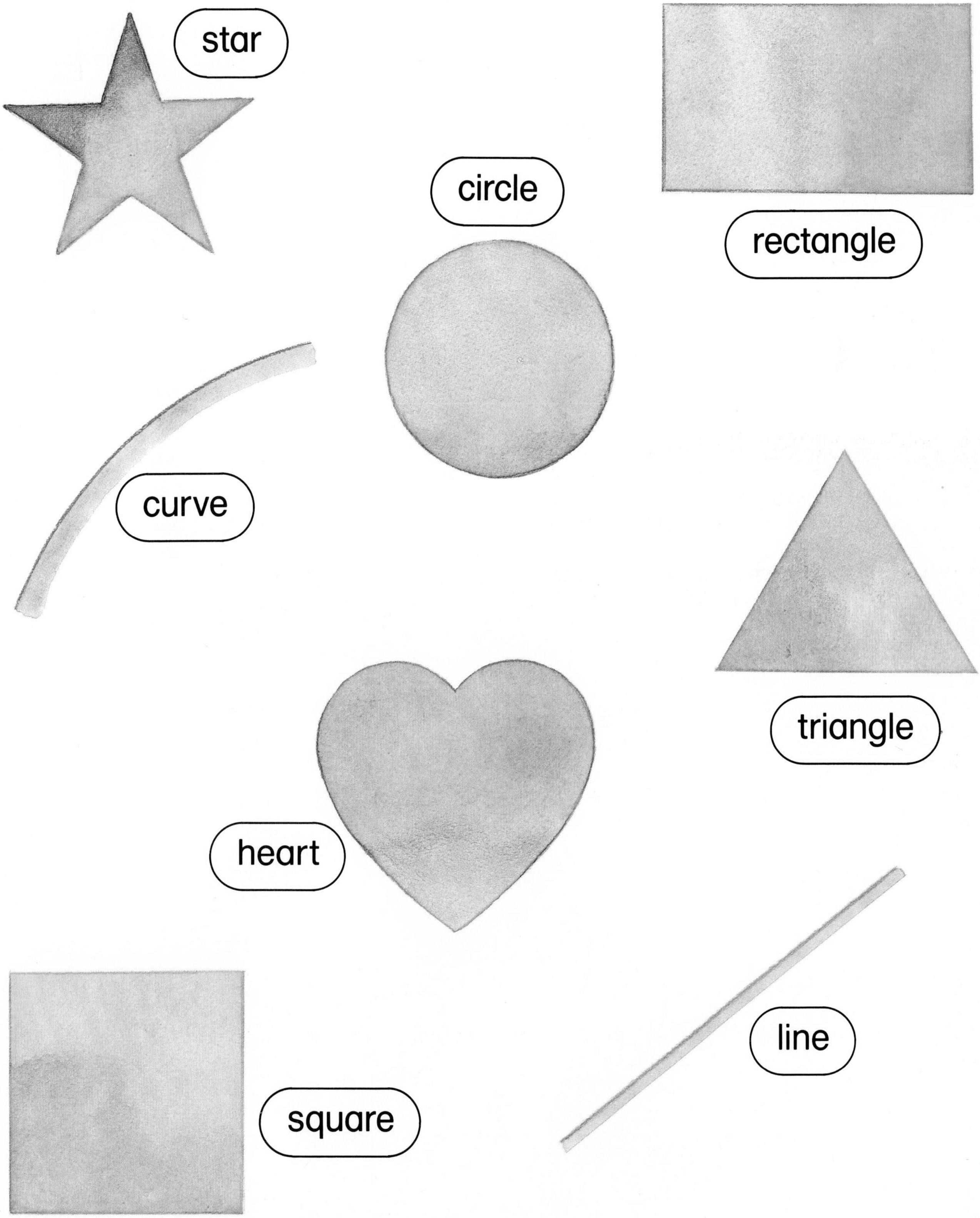

Numbers

0 zero

1 one

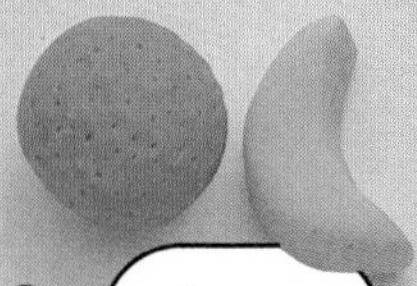

2 two

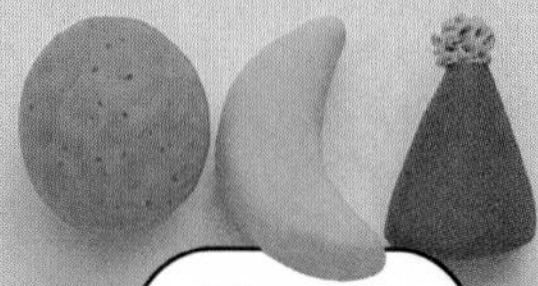

3 three

4 four

5 five

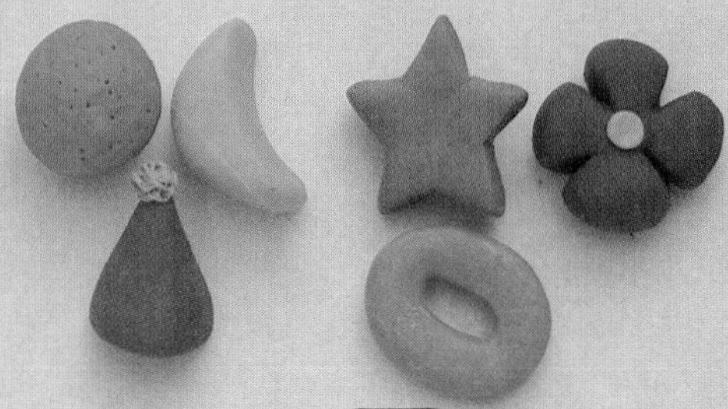

6 six

7 seven

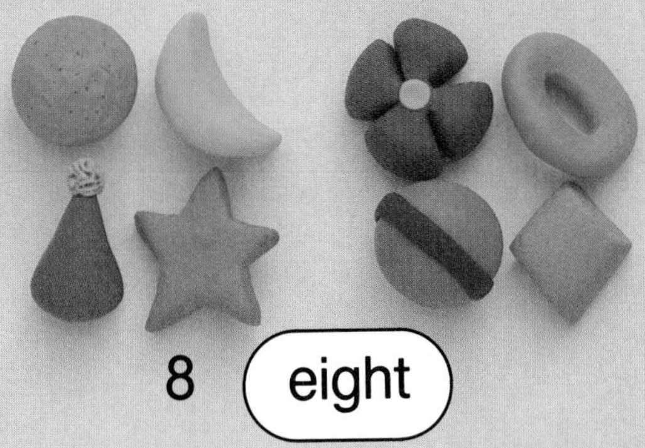

8 eight

9 nine

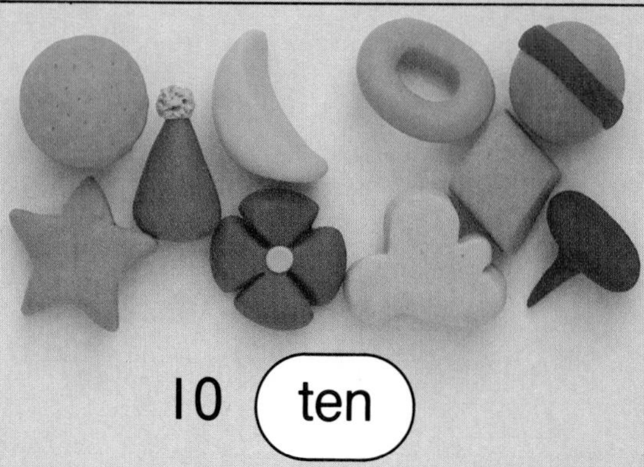

10 ten

Money

penny 1¢

pennies

nickel 5¢

dime 10¢

quarter 25¢

one dollar $1.00

five dollars $5.00

Months of the Year and Holidays

Valentine's Day

Months of the Year and Holidays

Seasons

Days of the Week and Time of Day

Sunday

Monday

Tuesday

Wednesday

Thursday

Friday

Saturday

morning

afternoon

night

Index

Index

Index

T t

Index

Artists

Pages 6–7—Dick Martin
Pages 8–19—Kees de Kiefte
Page 37—Alan Bernard
Pages 38–39—Chi Chung
Pages 40–49—Linda Kelen
Pages 50–59—Patti Boyd
Pages 60–65—Lane Yerkes
Pages 66–67—Blanche Sims
Pages 68–69—Lane Yerkes
Pages 70–73—Blanche Sims
Pages 74–75—Chi Chung
Pages 76–77—Chi Chung/Robert Masheris
Pages 78–79—Blanche Sims
Pages 80–85—Janet LaSalle
Pages 86–93—Lynn Adams
Pages 94–99—Dick Martin
Pages 100–101—Bob Knight
Pages 102–103—Chi Chung
Pages 104–105—Gioia Fiammenghi
Pages 106–107—Brian Karas
Pages 108–109—Robert Alley
Pages 110–111—Brian Karas
Pages 112–113—Robert Alley
Pages 114–115—Brian Karas
Pages 116–117—Gioia Fiammenghi
Pages 118–119—Roberta Collier
Pages 120–123—Carolyn Bracken
Pages 124–125—Roberta Collier
Pages 126–127—Julie Durrel
Pages 128–129—Robert Masheris
Page 130—Georgia Shola
Pages 132–133—Randall Enos
Pages 134–135—Andrea Eberbach

Photographers

Page 20—dog: Robert Carr/Bruce Coleman Inc.
puppy, goldfish: Zig Leszczynski/Animals Animals
puppies: Ginger Chih/Peter Arnold, Inc.
parakeet: Robert Pearcy/Animals Animals
parrot: Hans Reinhard/Bruce Coleman Inc.
Page 21—guinea pig, hamster: Hans Reinhard/Bruce Coleman Inc.
rabbit/bunny: Jane Burton/Bruce Coleman Inc.
cat & kitten: Robert Pearcy/Animals Animals
gerbil: E. R. Degginger/Bruce Coleman Inc.
Page 22—lamb & sheep: Grant Heilman/Grant Heilman Photography
sheep (plural), chickens: Hans Reinhard/Bruce Coleman Inc.
turkey, rooster: Ben Goldstein/Valenti Photography
hen: Richard Kolar/Animals Animals
chick: Robert Pearcy/Animals Animals
Page 23—cow & calf: Charlton Photos
pig/hog, goat: Hans Reinhard/Bruce Coleman Inc.
pony & colt: J. C. Allen & Son, Inc.
donkey: L. L. T. Rhodes/Animals Animals
Page 24—raccoon: Hans Reinhard/Bruce Coleman Inc.
groundhog, beaver: Wayne Lankinen/Bruce Coleman Inc.
wolf: Stephan J. Krasemann/DRK Photo
skunk: Bob & Clara Calhoun/Bruce Coleman Inc.
coyote: Wayne Lynch/DRK Photo
Page 25—chipmunk, squirrel: Zig Leszczynski/Animals Animals
fox: Breck P. Kent/Animals Animals
foxes: Hans Reinhard/Bruce Coleman Inc.
Page 26—porcupine: Kenneth W. Fink/Bruce Coleman Inc.
mouse: Breck P. Kent/Animals Animals
mice: Jane Burton/Bruce Coleman Inc.
deer: Tom Edwards/Animals Animals
deer (plural): Leonard Lee Rue III/Bruce Coleman Inc.
possum/opossum: Martin L. Stouffer/Animals Animals
Page 27—bat: Jane Burton/Bruce Coleman Inc.
polar bear: Johnny Johnson/Animals Animals
panda: J. L. G. Grande/Bruce Coleman Inc.
bear: Charles Palek/Animals Animals
rat: Hans Reinhard/Bruce Coleman Inc.
kangaroo: Patti Murray/Animals Animals
Page 28—turtle: Leonard Lee Rue III/Bruce Coleman Inc.
snake, lizard: Hans Reinhard/Bruce Coleman Inc.
alligator: C. C. Lockwood/DRK Photo
iguana: Alan Blank/Bruce Coleman Inc.
Page 29—spider: Stephen J. Krasemann/DRK Photo
fish: Zig Leszczynski/Animals Animals
lobster: Scott Johnson/Animals Animals
frog: Hans Reinhard/Bruce Coleman Inc.
toad: John Gerlach/DRK Photo
Page 30—seal: Alan G. Nelson/Animals Animals
octopus: Jane Burton/Bruce Coleman Inc.
walrus: Stephen J. Krasemann/DRK Photo
whale: C. Allan Morgan/Peter Arnold, Inc.
dolphin: Mickey Gibson/Animals Animals
Page 31—chimpanzee/ape: J. & D. Bartlett/Bruce Coleman Inc.
gorilla/ape: Hans Reinhard/Bruce Coleman Inc.
monkey: Rod Williams/Bruce Coleman Inc.
monkeys: Zig Leszczynski/Animals Animals
Page 32—lion: Charles Palek/Animals Animals
tiger: Zig Leszczynski/Animals Animals
leopard: Belinda Wright/DRK Photo
yak: Bruce Coleman/Bruce Coleman Inc.
camel: Mickey Gibson/Animals Animals
Page 33—giraffe: Stefan Meyers/Animals Animals
zebra: N. Myers/Bruce Coleman Inc.
elephant: Zig Leszczynski/Animals Animals
hippopotamus: Simon Trevor/Bruce Coleman Inc.
rhinoceros: Jane Burton/Bruce Coleman Inc.
Page 34—goose: Margot Conte/Animals Animals
geese: Henry R. Fox/Animals Animals
ostrich: Zig Leszczynski/Animals Animals
crow: Hans Reinhard/Bruce Coleman Inc.
blue jay: Breck P. Kent/Animals Animals
Page 35—eagle: Johnny Johnson/DRK Photo
owl, robin: E. R. Degginger/Animals Animals
hummingbird: Alan G. Nelson/Animals Animals
cardinal: Zig Leszczynski/Animals Animals
duck: Donald E. Waite/Bruce Coleman Inc.
Page 36—butterfly: Eric Dragesco/Bruce Coleman Inc.
ant: G. I. Bernard/Animals Animals
caterpillar: Breck P. Kent/Animals Animals
fly: Avril Ramage/O. S. F./Animals Animals
beetle: Hans Reinhard/Bruce Coleman Inc.
bee: Donald Specker/Animals Animals
Page 131—Scott, Foresman staff

The D'Nealian® Alphabet

a b c d e f g h i j

k l m n o p q r s

t u v w x y z

A B C D E F G H

I J K L M N O P

Q R S T U V W

X Y Z , ' . ?

1 2 3 4 5

6 7 8 9 10